· INTRODUCTION ·

The first time visitor to Liverpool is usually amazed by the grandeur of its architecture. A walk through the city centre to the waterfront reveals the impressive legacy of one of the world's greatest cities of the 19th century. The 'second city of Empire', it eclipsed London at times for its commerce. The miles of docks witnessed not only the shipping of cargoes to and from all corners of the globe but also a massive exodus of millions of emigrants from all over Europe seeking prosperity in the New World. Liverpool was an outward looking boom town expressing its confidence in fine buildings and impressive public spaces.

Today, the visitor might be surprised to know that Liverpool has more government-listed buildings than any other British city outside of London (and that it has more Georgian buildings than Bath). Yet, Liverpool is more than fine architecture. A city known worldwide as the birthplace of the Beatles, the home of Liverpool Football Club and famed for its vitality, humour and generosity, it even has its own unmistakable accent that reinforces its reputation as a unique place to visit and enjoy.

· THE RIVER & FERRIES ·

Liverpool's name is synonymous with the sea and ships and the best starting point for any tour is to take a ferry trip across the Mersey. Ferries were already well-established when Edward III granted the monks of Birkenhead Priory legal rights in 1330 and no visit to the city is complete without the experience of sailing out from under the twin turrets of the Royal Liver Building to take in the view from mid-river. However many times you make the short trip, there is always a sense of adventure and expectancy.

(Far left) The River Mersey
looking towards Birkenhead
(Left) Liverpool waterfront
(Right) Ferry 'cross the Mersey

· PIER HEAD ·

Dominating the waterfront are the three buildings at its centre; the Royal Liver Building, the Cunard Building and the Port of Liverpool Building. Monumental and magnificent, they stand in testimony to the enterprise and prosperity of Liverpool in the early years of this century.

The Royal Liver Building is probably the city's best known landmark. Standing 322 feet from the ground to the top of the legendary Liver Birds, it was the first large-scale reinforced concrete building in the world. Designed by W Aubrey Thomas, it has an originality and power that is unique in Britain.

(Left) Pier Head at night
(Right) Mersey ferry

The Tate Gallery, centre for contemporary art

Albert Dock from Canning Dock

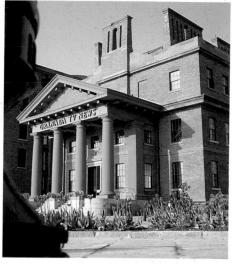

The cast-iron portico of the Dock Traffic Office,
now part of Granada Television

· ALBERT DOCK ·

Albert Dock is Liverpool's greatest expression of dock architecture. The vast warehouse complex was opened by Prince Albert in 1846. The architect, Yorkshire engineer Jesse Hartley, introduced the closed dock system, of which Albert Dock was the prototype. The closed dock system ensured greater protection of valuable cargoes such as tobacco and spirits.

Built predominantely of cast-iron and brick, with external walls four feet thick at ground level, the Albert Dock has both simplicity and enormous power. Although it marked an important step forward in the design of docks, it soon became obsolete with the introduction of larger steam-powered ships. By 1920, it had virtually ceased to be used for commercial activities.

Fortunately, the buildings have survived virtually intact. Now the largest group of Grade One listed buildings in the country, Albert Dock has been sensitively restored to house an exciting mix of shops, businesses, museums and galleries and is one of Britain's top tourist attractions.

Merseyside Maritime Museum is housed in one block with five floors of shipping-related exhibitions and further exhibits in the quayside buildings outside including an important new section devoted to the history of Liverpool. Adjacent to it is the Tate Gallery, the major centre for contemporary art in the North of England. Elsewhere in the complex, The Beatles Story is an essential attraction for fans of Liverpool's most famous export.

· COMMERCE ·

As the port expanded and Liverpool grew in prosperity, many of the companies associated with the port erected buildings to reflect their importance and confidence.

A short walk up Water Street and along Castle Street will give a taste of some of the finest commercial architecture in the country. Particularly worth looking at is the glass-facaded Oriel Chambers, a building so far ahead of its time that its architect, Peter Ellis, was ridiculed to the extent that he designed no further buildings. On the opposite side of Water Street stands

(Far left) The city viewed from the Royal Liver Building
(Left) Holt Arcade, running the length of India Buildings
(Above) The impressive interior of Martins Bank (now Barclays Bank) in Water Street

the impressive India Buildings, with a shopping arcade named after the Holt family, who built the block as headquarters for their shipping line.

The same architect, Herbert J Rowse, was responsible for the magnificent Martin's Bank Building (now Barclays Bank) across the road. Completed in 1932, it is his finest work with a superb interior which can be viewed during the bank's opening times.

Next door to the bank stands the Town Hall, built between 1749 and 1754 to the design of John Wood of Bath. A disastrous fire in 1795 necessitated a reconstruction of parts of the building by James Wyatt, who added the impressive dome on its high drum. The interior contains magnificent civic suites complete with fine period furniture.

(Left) The Town Hall, one of the finest Georgian public buildings in England
(Above) The graceful cast-iron windows of Oriel Chambers, the most remarkable office building of its time

· CULTURE ·

Liverpool's most important building architecturally is St George's Hall. Described as the finest Greco-Roman building in Europe, St George's Hall was designed by 24 year old Harvey Lonsdale Elmes, who gained his commission by winning a competition to design a building to house a music festival. Liverpool Town Council then held a second competition for assize courts, which Elmes also won. The Corporation decided to combine the two schemes and St George's Hall is the result.

Work started in 1842 but Elmes, dying from tubercolosis in 1847, was

(Far left) The south facade of St George's Hall, the greatest classical monument of the nineteenth century
(Left) The Small Concert Hall, considered by many to be the finest room in the building

unable to see his masterpiece completed. His friend and
mentor C R Cockerell was brought in to finish the
building and was responsible for designing the
exquisite Small Concert Hall.

Few buildings can match the grandeur of St George's
Hall. Its position, on spacious St George's Plateau
overlooked by the Gothic splendour of the old North
Western Hotel, enhances the monumental quality of the
building and rewards the visitor arriving from Lime
Street Station with a remarkable first impression of the
city.

(Right) The entrance of the Walker Art Gallery
flanked by Raphael and Michaelangelo
(Below) The semi- circular facade of Picton
Reading Room

The view from St George's Plateau reveals a striking sweep of classical buildings. Here, on William Brown Street, Liverpool Museum, William Brown Library and the Walker Art Gallery rub shoulders with each other, offering a superb choice of internationally important collections. The Walker Art Gallery, in particular, is widely regarded as having the most comprehensive collection of European art outside of London.

Two other features are worth noting. The Wellington Column stands 132 feet high and is an exact replica of the Melville Monument in Edinburgh. It is said that the statue of the Duke is cast in metal from guns captured at Waterloo. At the foot of the monument is the Steble Fountain, erected in 1879.

(Above) St George's Plateau; the finest civic panorama in Britain.

· THE CATHEDRALS ·

Liverpool is one of few cities to boast two cathedrals. Both were built this century although you would hardly be likely to find two greater contrasts in style. Paradoxically, the Anglican Cathedral was designed by a Catholic, 21 year old Giles Gilbert Scott and the Metropolitan Cathedral by a Protestant, Frederick Gibbard.

Liverpool Cathedral is one of the largest cathedrals in the world; a massive, red sandstone masterpiece which took nearly 75 years to complete. Commanding a superb site, high above the river, the Cathedral was the first to be consecrated in England on a wholly new site since the 13th century.

(Far left) Two Cathedrals on opposite sides of Hope Street
(Below left) The High Altar, Liverpool Cathedral
(Below right) Interior, Metropolitan Cathedral

At the other end of appropriately-named Hope Street stands the Metropolitan Cathedral. Built in a mere five years and completed in 1967, its imaginative conical shape reveals an interior of astonishing light and colour.

Together, the two cathedrals dominate the landscape; communicating a powerful spirit of ecumenicalism for which the city has become famous in recent years.

(Above left) Liverpool Cathedral
viewed from the Georgian elegance
of Rodney Street
(Above right) The Metropolitan
Cathedral of Christ the King

· GEORGIAN LIVERPOOL ·

Liverpool retains a large part of its Georgian heritage. Although a considerable amount has been lost this century, many of the remaining buildings have been sensitively restored particularly in the Rodney Street/Canning Street area.

Rodney Street was one of the first of the new residential streets created by Liverpool's wealthy merchants created at the end of the eighteenth century. Today, the street still captures the elegance of an earlier Liverpool; the buildings are beautifully proportioned and sit side by side in harmony, enhanced by subtle differences in door styles, railings and other features. Little wonder that both the University of Liverpool and the John Moores University are based here in the extensive network of streets and squares that run between the dominant features of the city's two cathedrals.

Doors, Rodney Street

(Left) Elegant houses in
Falkner Square
(Above) Abercromby Square with its
central gazebo is now an elegant part
of the University

· THE ARTS ·

Liverpool has a long tradition of excellence in the arts. The internationally renowned Royal Liverpool Philharmonic Orchestra has its permanent home in Hope Street and, further down the street, is the Everyman Theatre, a pioneering repertory company housed in a converted Gospel Hall. Claiming seniority as Britain's longest established repertory theatre, the Playhouse in Williamson Square has long been an important contributor to the city's artistic reputation. Two commercial theatres, the Empire and Royal Court, regularly stage national touring companies and shows. The Tate Gallery in the Albert Dock, the John Moores Exhibition at the Walker, and the Bluecoat Gallery have ensured Liverpool's standing for contemporary visual art.

The city has gained a deserved reputation for its artistic energy. The energy released by the Beatles revealed a city of musicians, poets, actors, playwrights and painters. Today, this creative diversity continues to make its mark in every area of the national arts scene.

Royal Liverpool Philharmonic Orchestra
in concert

Liverpool Playhouse, Williamson Square

(Left) The Empire Theatre, Lime Street

(Left) Croxteth Hall, the family home of the Earls of Sefton, now owned by the City of Liverpool

(Right) The Palm House, Sefton Park

· THE PARKS ·

Liverpool has a great heritage of public parks and gardens, many of which were the former estates of merchants and shipping owners. The Victorians heralded a golden era of public park design and Liverpool was in the forefront of the movement to recreate a breath of the country in the townscape. Princes Park, in 1842, was the first independent commission for the master of landscape design, Joseph Paxton, and was a benchmark for public park design in Europe and America.

Particularly worth visiting are Sefton Park, with its graceful avenues, wooded vales, lake and Palm House and the more formal Calderstones Park with its walled Old English Garden, Japanese Garden and other specialist areas.

(Above) Calderstones Park
and Mansion
(Above right) The Field of Hope,
Sefton Park
(Right) Speke Hall, one of the finest
timber-framed buildings in Britain,
now owned by the National Trust

· THE CITY CENTRE ·

Liverpool city centre is an interesting mix of old and new. The oldest is the Bluecoat Chambers, a lovely Queen Anne building which is also the first art centre in Britain. The complex contains a gallery, concert room, studios and shops and has an exquisite enclosed garden.

In contrast, the new shopping developments in Clayton

(Left) Detail of Compton's Building, one of many fine Victorian buildings in the shopping area

(Above) Bluecoat Chambers, a beautiful example of Queen Anne style building, now a major art centre

(Far right) Liverpool has the oldest established Chinese community in Europe

(Right) The magnificent gates of the Philharmonic Hotel, one of many superb period public houses

Square and Cavern Walks are interesting additions to the city's architecture.

Pedestrianisation, the restoration of important buildings including the Lyceum on Bold Street and other improvements are transforming the centre. Liverpool has the oldest Chinese community in Europe and their area is being upgraded. Elsewhere, around London Road, Queen Square and Bold Street, ambitious schemes are underway, bringing new life to the city.

· THE BEATLES ·

To the outsider, perhaps, more than anything else, Liverpool is the birthplace of the Beatles. Over thirty years ago, they burst into the consciousness of the world in a way no other group had done before, captivating young people everywhere.

Today, guided tours around the Beatles' old haunts are an essential part of any fan's itinerary, taking in the homes and birthplaces, schools and early meeting places. The wrought iron gates of Strawberry Fields and the 'shelter in the middle of the roundabout' in Penny Lane are particularly popular as is the excellent 'Beatles Story' at the Albert Dock.

(Above) 251 Menlove Avenue, where John Lennon spent much of his childhood

(Right) The Beatles Story, a fascinating exhibition at Albert Dock

(Above) The gates to Strawberry Fields

· SPORT ·

It is said that sport is a religion in Liverpool. In particular, football dominates conversation. Liverpool Football Club is the most successful in Britain and a tour around their ground is obligatory for those interested in football. Everton FC have been somewhat overshadowed by their close neighbour in recent years although few other clubs can match their record of league title and cup wins.

Over 150 years ago, a steeplechase took place over an arduous four mile course. Later called the Grand National, the race has held centre stage in the racing calendar. No other sporting event attracts such nationwide attention as the large field of horses and riders tackle a course of unrelenting severity.

The city has a fine reputation for other sports including rugby union, boxing, cycling and athletics. The City Council has been active in providing top quality facilities and these are ensuring that Liverpool's sporting traditions continue to develop.

The Grand National, Aintree

Liverpool v Everton, the highlight of every season

The Kop, Anfield, home of Liverpool Football Club

· THE POOL OF LIFE ·

If Liverpool did not exist, it would have to be invented' commented one favourably impressed visitor at the turn of the century. What other city can offer such magnificent architecture, so many great galleries and museums and such a diversity of activities? Liverpool is a remarkable city with a vibrancy and enthusiasm that never fails to impress. In the words of the great psychologist, Carl Jung, 'Liverpool is the Pool of Life'.

LIVERPOOL
The Pool of Life

Design and Artwork by H J Thomas (051 734 3559)
Text by Colin Wilkinson Typesetting by Typebase Limited
Photography by: Stephen Brock, John Calderbank, Ron Davies, Peter Hagerty, Steve Hale, Ron Jones,
Alex Laing, Christian Smith, Peter Whitfield, David Williams

Published by The Bluecoat Press, Bluecoat Chambers, Liverpool (051 707 2390)